PIANO · VOCAL · GUITAR

BOHEMIAN RHAPSODY

MUSIC FROM THE MOTION PICTURE SOUNDTRACK

ISBN 978-1-5400-4056-5

HAL•LEONARD®

Visit Hal Leonard Online at
www.halleonard.com

Contact Us:
Hal Leonard
7777 West Bluemound Road
Milwaukee, WI 53213
Email: info@halleonard.com

In Europe contact:
Hal Leonard Europe Limited
42 Wigmore Street
Marylebone, London, W1U 2RN
Email: info@halleonardeurope.com

In Australia contact:
Hal Leonard Australia Pty. Ltd.
4 Lentara Court
Cheltenham, Victoria, 3192 Australia
Email: info@halleonard.com.au

CONTENTS

TWENTIETH CENTURY FOX TRADEMARK

Composed by
ALFRED NEWMAN

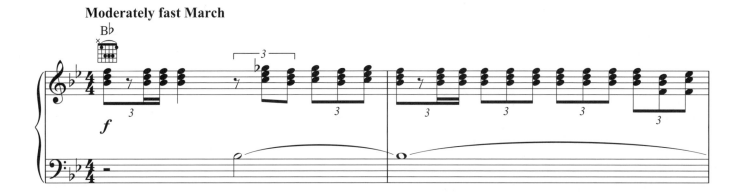

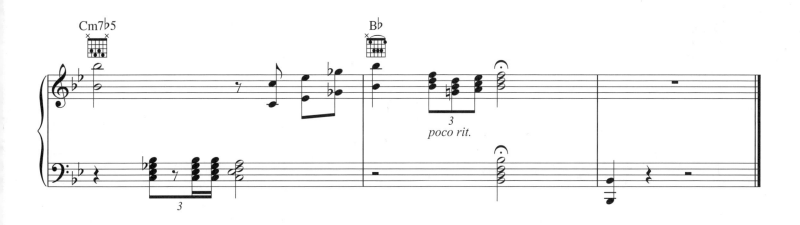

SOMEBODY TO LOVE

Words and Music by
FREDDIE MERCURY

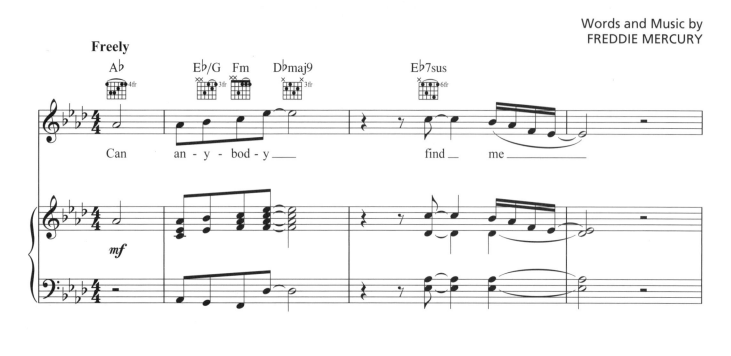

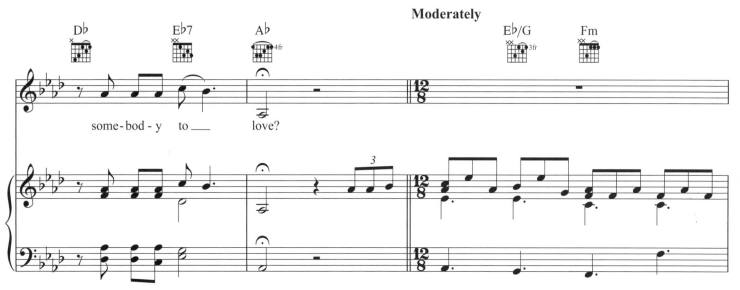

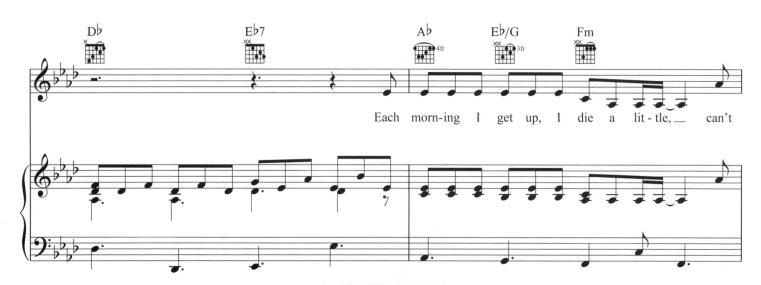

face _____ no de - feat. I just got - ta get out of this pris - on cell, __ one

day I'm gon - na be free, Lord. _____ Find me some - bod - y to love, __

find me some - bod - y to love, ____ find me some - bod - y to love, __

find me some - bod - y to love, ____ find me some - bod - y to love, __

DOING ALL RIGHT

Words and Music by BRIAN MAY
and TIM STAFFELL

14

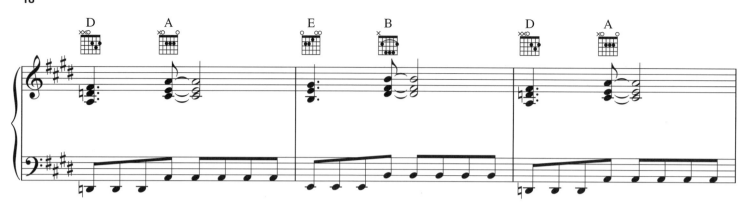

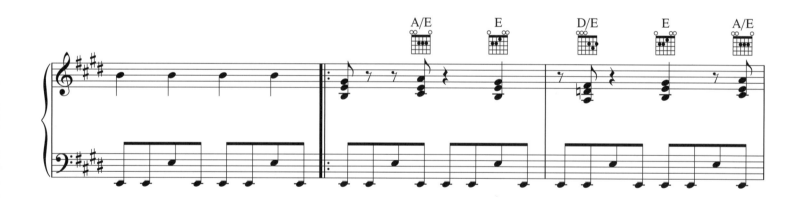

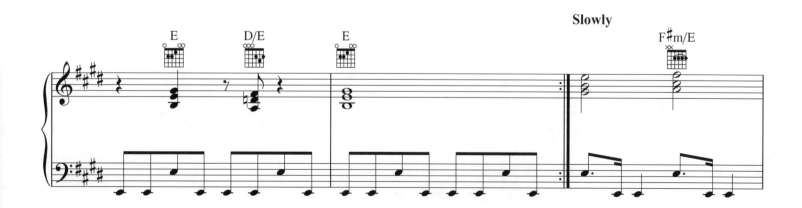

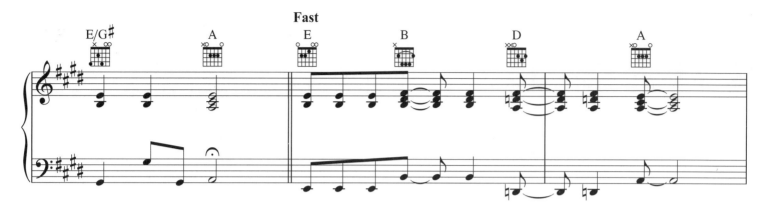

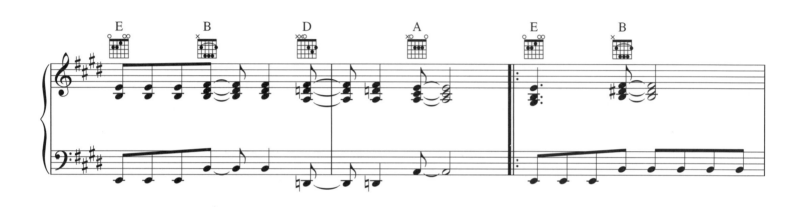

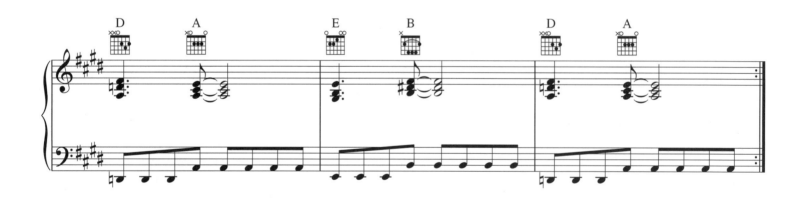

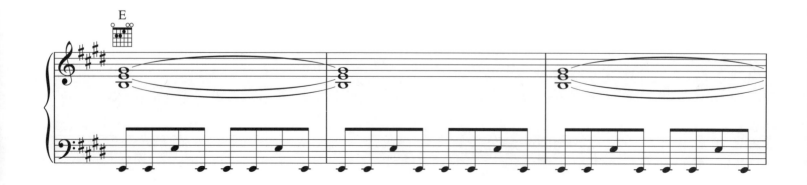

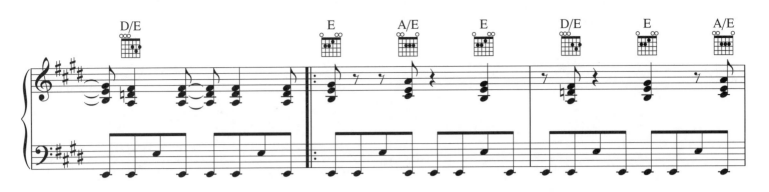

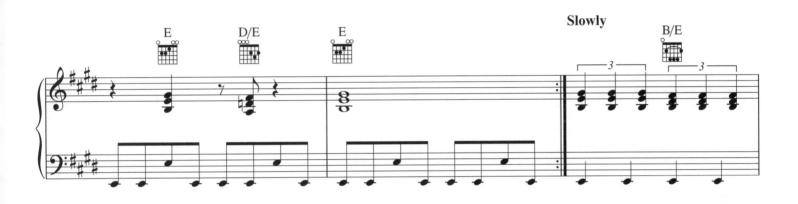

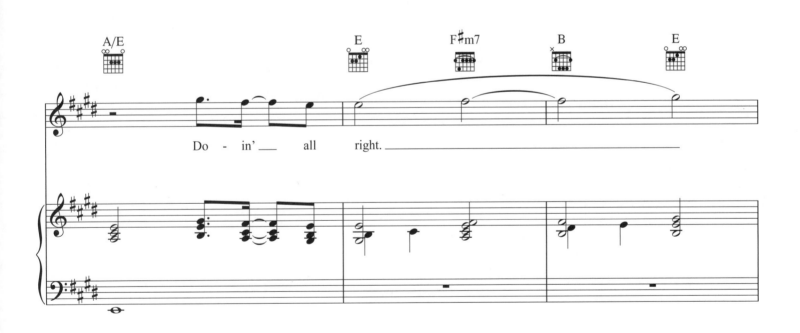

Do - in' __ all right. _____

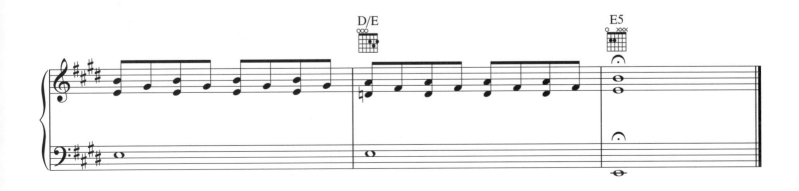

KEEP YOURSELF ALIVE

Words and Music by
BRIAN MAY

Keep your-self a - live. _ It -'ll take you all your time and a-mon-ey, hon - ey, you'll sur - vive.

Keep your-self a - live, keep your-self a - live. _ It -'ll take you all your time and a-mon-ey to

KILLER QUEEN

Words and Music by
FREDDIE MERCURY

sa - tia - ble an ap - pe - tite, wan-na try. _____

To a -

Drop of a hat she's as will - ing as play - ful as a pus - sy - cat, then

mo - men - tar - i - ly out of ac - tion, tem - po - rar - i - ly out of gas; to

FAT BOTTOMED GIRLS

Words and Music by
BRIAN MAY

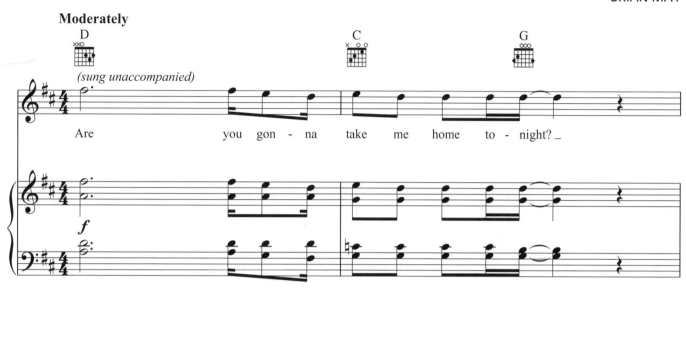

BOHEMIAN RHAPSODY

Words and Music by
FREDDIE MERCURY

Slowly

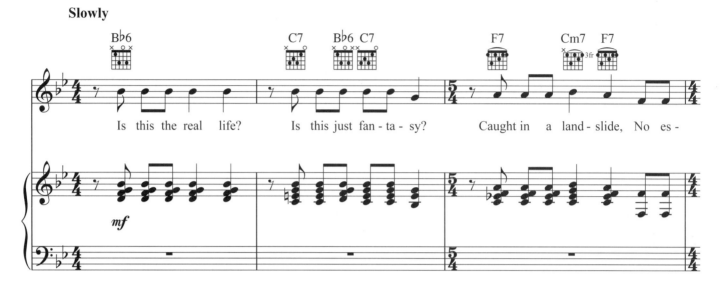

Is this the real life? Is this just fan-ta-sy? Caught in a land-slide, No es-

cape from re-al-i-ty. O-pen your eyes, Look up to the skies and

see, I'm just a poor boy, I need no sym-pa-thy, Be-cause I'm

38

all.

I see a lit-tle sil-hou-et-to of a man, Scar-a-

L'istesso tempo (♪ = ♩)

NOW I'M HERE

Words and Music by
BRIAN MAY

love you so. _____

Don't I

Go, go, go, _____ lit - tle queen - ie.

Repeat and Fade

CRAZY LITTLE THING CALLED LOVE

Words and Music by
FREDDIE MERCURY

mo - tor bike — un - til I'm read - y. Cra - zy lit - tle thing called

love.

mo - tor bike ___ un - til I'm read - y. Cra - zy lit - tle thing called

love. This thing ___ called

love, I ___ just ___ can't ___ han - dle it. ___ This

thing called love, I ___ must ___ get a -

round to it. ___ I ain't ___ read - y. Cra - zy lit - tle thing called

love, cra - zy lit - tle thing called love, cra -

- zy lit - tle thing called love, cra - zy lit - tle thing called

love, hey, cra - zy lit - tle thing called love.

LOVE OF MY LIFE

Words and Music by
FREDDIE MERCURY

WE WILL ROCK YOU

Words and Music by
BRIAN MAY

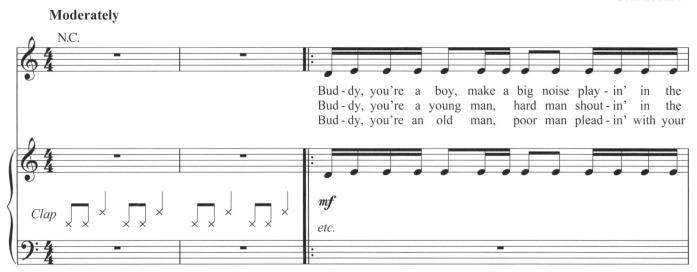

Bud - dy, you're a boy, make a big noise play - in' in the
Bud - dy, you're a young man, hard man shout - in' in the
Bud - dy, you're an old man, poor man plead - in' with your

street. Gon - na be a big man some - day. You got mud on yo' face, you big dis - grace,
street. Gon - na take on the world some - day. You got blood on yo' face, you big dis - grace,
eyes. Gon - na make you some peace some - day. You got mud on your face, you big dis - grace. Some -

kick - in' your can all o - ver the place. Sing - in'
wav - in' your ban - ner all o - ver the place. Sing - in' } we will, we will rock you. ____
bod - y bet - ter put you back in - to your place. Sing - in'

ANOTHER ONE BITES THE DUST

Words and Music by
JOHN DEACON

Steve walks war-i-ly down __ the street with the
How do you think I'm going to get a-long with-
There are plen-ty of ways you can hurt __ a man and

brim pulled way down low. __ Ain't no sound but the sound of his feet; __ ma-
out you, when you're gone? __ You took me for ev-'ry-thing that I had __ and
bring him to the ground. __ You can beat him, you can cheat him, you can treat him bad __ and

chine guns read-y to go. __ Are you read-y, hey! __ Are you read-y for this? __ Are you
kicked me out on my own. __ Are you hap-py? Are you sat-is-fied? How
leave him when he's down. __ But I'm read-y, yes I'm read-y for you. __ I'm

67

I WANT TO BREAK FREE

Words and Music by
JOHN DEACON

I want to break free. _____ I want to break

free.
love.
on.

I want to break free from your lies. You're so
I've fall-en in love for the first time, and
I can't get used to liv-ing with-out, liv-ing with-out,

UNDER PRESSURE

Words and Music by FREDDIE MERCURY,
JOHN DEACON, BRIAN MAY,
ROGER TAYLOR and DAVID BOWIE

Additional Lyrics

2. Chippin' around,
   Kick my brains around the floor.
   These are the days it never rains but it pours.
   (Vocal ad lib.)
   People on streets.
   People on streets.

WHO WANTS TO LIVE FOREVER

Words and Music by
BRIAN MAY

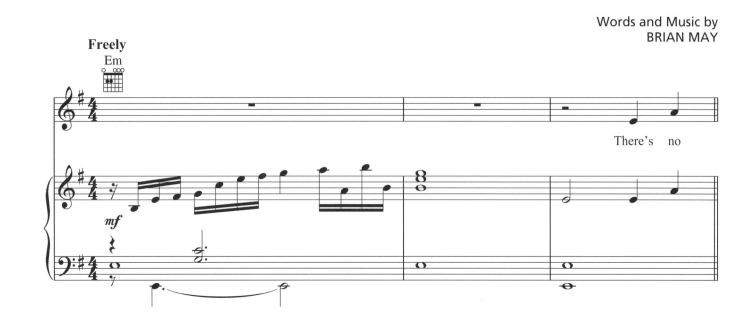

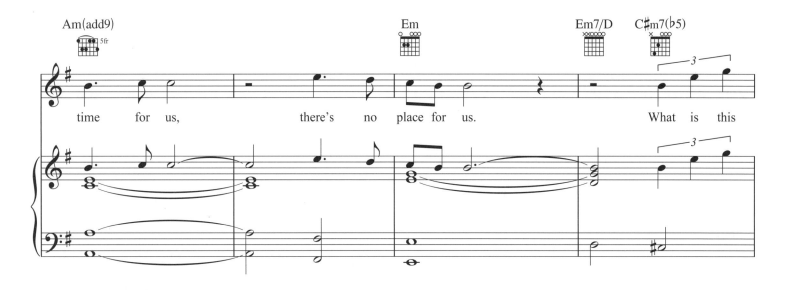

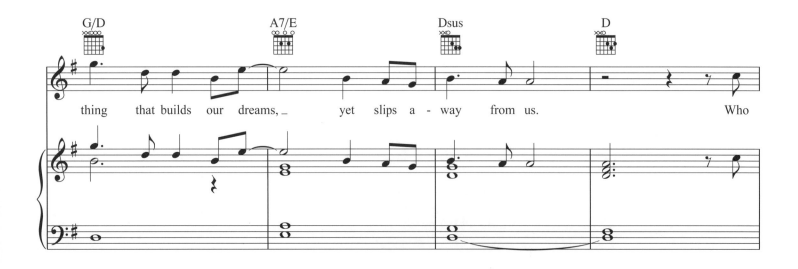

THE SHOW MUST GO ON

Words and Music by FREDDIE MERCURY,
BRIAN MAY, ROGER TAYLOR
and JOHN DEACON

Ooh, I'll top the bill, __ I'll o-ver-kill, __ I have to find the will __ to car-ry on, __

show. _____

Repeat and Fade

RADIO GA GA

Words and Music by
ROGER TAYLOR

HAMMER TO FALL

Words and Music by
BRIAN MAY

Ba - by, now __ your strug - gle's all in vain. __

WE ARE THE CHAMPIONS

Words and Music by
FREDDIE MERCURY

DON'T STOP ME NOW

Words and Music by
FREDDIE MERCURY

Slowly

To - night __ I'm gon - na have my - self _____ a real good time. I feel a-
(D.C.) Da da da da da (etc.)

live, _____ and the world

turn - ing in - side out, yeah, __ and float - ing a - round __ in